TOUCHING SEDONA

SPEAKS OF MANY TRUTHS THROUGH

ROBERT SHAPIRO

LIGHT TECHNOLOGY
SHIRT POCKET BOOKS

Touching Sedona

Speaks of Many Truths through

Robert Shapiro

Light Technology Publishing

ISBN 1-891824-47-3

Published by

Light Technology Publishing
PO Box 3540
Flagstaff, AZ 68003
1-800-450-0985
www.lighttechnology.com

Printed by

GraphTech
DIGITAL & PRINTING

4030 E. Huntington Dr.
Flagstaff, AZ 86004
1-928-526-1345

Table of Contents

1 Honoring the Red Rock: How to Cultivate Wisdom through Touch 1

2 Rock Wisdom and the Colors of the Earth 11

3 Communing with Gray Rock 13

4 Beige-Colored Rock and Children 17

5 Remembering with Dark Brown Rock 21

6 The Significance of Color 25

7 Soft White Rock, Strong Feelings 27

8 The Power of White Crystals 33

9 Finding What's Lost or Hidden with Blue Stone 37

10 A History Lesson with Black Rock 41

11 Green Wisdom 43

12 Pink: The Color of Love Unattainable 47

13 Creator Gold 51

14 Dreaming in Purple 55

15 All the Colors of the World 59

16 Water's Feminine Reflection 61

17 Rocks by the Sea and Inner Insight 65

18 Touching Sedona 67
19 A Benevolent Offering 71
Appendix A: Sedona Rock Beings 73

1
Honoring the Red Rock: How to Cultivate Wisdom through Touch

This is Speaks of Many Truths. Greetings. There are ways to relate to Sedona that are traditional and have not been discussed in print. Certain sacred people who used to come to this part of the world interacted with the different colors of stone and native plants. One of the things not very well understood in your time, even when your anthropologists have been exposed to traditional peoples, is the coloring of human faces and bodies.

Traditional peoples are mystical. One group who used to come here (usually the mystical men of that group) to learn something or teach something, one or the other, would go to be near the rock that they felt could support what they were teaching or learning. The rock, having been there for so long, would contain a significant amount of wisdom simply from its experience: what it felt, what it saw in its own way, what it had experienced of the knowledge the person was seeking.

In order to be more acceptable to the rock—so that the rock would feel that the mystical man was honoring it and acting in such a way as to create a greater communion—what the mystical man would do is make a paste or a paint that would stick to his own body (maybe the face, maybe the chest, maybe the arms, sometimes the legs between the knee and thigh, whatever he could reach) and spread this color on himself as long as it contained some rock dust of that color. In this way, he was not trying to disguise himself as the rock—because the man would know that the rock would know who he was—but he was attempting to honor the rock. He was saying in rock language (which is not mental but physical), "I honor you. I ask for your guidance, your assistance and your wisdom to the degree you would like to give it."

Then he would take some portion of his body colored with the rock dust and touch it to the rock with very specific touches—sometimes just leaning against the rock—and ask the rock to commune to him any wisdom it might have. For instance, if it was a rock associated with altitude, maybe he would want to know something about birds or the sky. If, on the other hand, it was the red rock that Sedona is known for, perhaps he would want to know something about thoughts, dreams and stories, because the red rock [sandstone] in Sedona is not very firm and dissolves gradually, turning to dust that is blown around. This is because the red rock contains the spark of thoughts, ideas that stimulate stories of benefit to people all over the world. It would be possible to feel what you were going to be given—a dream or a vision or perhaps a story—or to be telling a story that you already knew and discover you have a new ending for it. Maybe that is stimulated by the rock.

If we think of a modern radio station that broadcasts signals or stories or information as far as they can go, this is really a technical imitation of what the wind has always done. The wind takes stories, energies in the form of some substance, and carries them all over the world. Sometimes seeds of plants are carried across the sea and released over a continent where the plant might be needed someday. Maybe it isn't needed now, but it might be needed five thousand years from now, because then animals will migrate to that area and need the food those seeds can bring. In five thousand years, the plant will re-create itself many times. When the animal comes, it will be there.

For years and years, the wind has been doing this. So why not think of it like this: You could wait for the wind to deposit some of that dust where you live, or if you are in Sedona, you could go to this or that rock. You could touch it in some honorable way. You could even take a little dust and touch it to your skin. In this case, because you want to honor the rock and you want something from it, you would put that dust on the back of your hand. If you put it on the palm of your hand . . . that's what you give and take with. Here you are asking to receive something. It is not something you are giving or taking; it is a request. Since it is a request, a gentle approach is needed. Put it on the back of your left hand, the feminine hand, and gently touch it to the rock. As you are touching the rock, ask your question or make your request.

And then sit there and meditate and just allow yourself to receive?

Meditate, or if that is not your way, just wait for as long as you feel comfortable. Then thank the rock. Even if you have no conscious thoughts, if nothing has changed, say thank you. Either the rock will reach out to you in your dreams at some point in your life, or it will help to stimulate the vision or request you have made when it can. This is also a way to remind people that what they desire, especially in the form of wisdom, can be granted through what Zoosh likes to call the divine physical.

When you become intimate with the divine physical, it becomes first nature. First nature is what you do; second nature is what you learn or think about and then do. When physicality is first nature, as in my time, then you do many things first, and later, when you get old enough to learn from grandfather or grandmother or your parents or maybe your uncles or aunts, you are shown how to do all the things you are doing in ways that will work better for you and others. But in the first few years of life, you do what you do on the basis of imitation. Later you are shown how.

So what I am saying is that in your time things are not so physical, because the mental has been raised to a high standard. Now people are very often afraid to touch. How often is a child told not to touch? And yet for us, unless something is genuinely dangerous or could be harmed by touching, it is not only allowed but encouraged. Look at the animals. It is in their nature to understand something, what it means to them, by using their senses. And very often this involves touching or tasting or even chewing a little bit: "What does that taste like? What must it be?" Human beings are very much like the animals and have similar abilities, so touch is important.

Is there anything different about touching, different things to ask for at different places?

Before you get to Sedona, write down some of the questions you have. If you live there, you can do this at home. Let the questions be in areas of life that interest you. If you are a youngster, ask simple questions: "What will I be like when I grow up?" If you are a little older, say, "What does this mean?" or you can even make a request, saying, "I'd like to know more about . . ." and then fill in the blank. It's best to ask for wisdom, because in its own way the stone will have seen much of human experience and migration and also will have seen and overheard many talks of spirit. Also, the stone is part of Mother Earth's body, so it will have the ability (maybe some stones better than others) to feel through Mother Earth's total knowledge what her answer would be to your question.

So you might as a youngster say, "What might I be like when I grow up?" or "Which one of my strengths should I work on the most?"—something more, a more specific question. Go around Sedona with your parents, if you are a youngster, or on your own, if you are more grown up. Then follow the procedure. Find a rock or maybe a rock face or some soil place—not a soil that people walk on all the time, but it could be a place where wild animals walk. Wild animals have natural wisdom and aren't dependent on humans for what they need.

Go to a rock—it might be a boulder or a rock face. If it's away from where everybody goes, good, but you don't have to go to some place strange or hard to reach. Then see if you can find some rock dust or even some pulverized rock (you don't have to pulverize it; it's always there in the cracks) that's the color of the rock you want to touch. Put it on the back of your left hand, and touch it to the rock. Ask your question out loud. If there are people around, you can whisper it, but say it out loud so the rock will know and understand that this is something that you want to know physically or consciously.

If you just think it, the rock might give you what you ask for to the extent of its ability, but it will be mixed in with all your other thoughts and you might not notice it. You want to dream about it. You want to have a vision or a picture or a sudden idea or inspiration that won't come only from the rock. By asking the rock, which is asking Mother Earth, you will then be able to feel that you are participating in the growth of your own wisdom and strength as an Earth person.

One of the rarest things in your time is for people to think of themselves as Earth people. If you're from Boston, you think of yourself as from that city. Or maybe you're from Mexico and you think of yourself as a citizen of that country. But rarely do you think of yourselves as Earth people, and yet from what I have seen or heard, people from other planets who visit call us Earth people. They don't say Sedona-ites, they don't say French people; they say Earth people.

One of the first ways we will show them we are Earth people is by treating our Mother Earth with the affection and trust and faith she shows us every day by sharing her body with us. This is a way we can be affectionate with her. Grandfathers and grandmothers like more than anything to have their grandchildren ask them questions when they are around, and I think maybe Mother Earth has this same attitude toward her children.

Do you have to walk up to where there is an outcropping from Mother Earth, or can you do this with a piece of rock you have?

It is best at an outcropping. If you have a piece of rock, it is hard to say who might have touched it. If you have picked it up from where it was starting its life—meaning a shard of rock, not a piece of river pebble—that might be all right. But probably most rocks, especially rounded ones, have tumbled or traveled; they are far away from where they were and might have been touched by many people. As such it is best to touch the rock where it is growing or connected to the Earth.

What about sitting on it? In many places, especially here in Sedona, you tend to sit on a rock.

No. It is always done with the back of your left hand.

Standing up?

Oh, you can be sitting if you wish, but I think that would be awkward. Probably you would be standing or crouching down or something.

Well, I was thinking about Bell Rock. If you were sitting on it, could you put your left hand on . . .

No. If you are sitting on it, then it confuses the rock, because the back of your hand is not just like a wire or a terminal. It is a part of your body that represents something. And if you are sitting on the rock, that part of your body represents something also, but it is not about asking for visions or dreams.

So the back of your left hand represents asking for visions or dreams?

Yes, the back of your hand is not arbitrary. It is specific.

2
Rock Wisdom and the Colors of the Earth

Is touching Boynton Canyon rock different from touching Cathedral Rock? Can we tie it into the vortexes?

Let's deal with colors first. Think of some of the places where rock is available for people to touch. If it is in the vortex places, fine, but it might be someplace where there is no vortex. Why not have people go to places besides the vortexes? Is Sedona just a place of vortexes, or is it something else?

Ultimately, of course, we want to encourage people to become more intimate with the land where they live. Those who cannot come to Sedona can try touching the different colors of rock where they live. For instance, people who have accessibility to rocks that are touched by the sea will have a completely different experience. Say a wave comes over a rock regularly—maybe every eighth or ninth wave—and the rock gets wet but you can still touch it. You might go over and ask the rock questions similar to what you would ask of any other color, but the answer will be completely different. This is because the rock learns not only from the wind—the wind delivers knowledge, wisdom and stories from all over—but it also gets knowledge and wisdom from the sea. So it might have more and different things to say.

That's beautiful. You could ask the sand that you're sitting on?

That's right. The more we learn about the intimacies of communication from Mother Earth and what her makeup is, the more we learn to appreciate her as she is. And the less we try to make her into something that makes sense to us.

3
Communing with Gray Rock

In the Sedona area, you can find red rock and beige rock and limestone, but mostly different colors of brown. There's no black granite or white marble or blue or anything. It's just mostly beige and red. Is it true that each color has a different type of wisdom to give?

Let's say the mystical man or budding mystical student wishes to connect with the gray rock that you have here, some of which is more accessible than others. The procedure will be the same in terms of putting some of the dust on the back of your left hand and touching the rock. It will always be the same unless I tell you something different.

The gray rock is about solidified thoughts, not unlike what is loosely termed gray matter by your scientists. But the thought is so solidified within the gray

rock that you will need to jar it loose—not by striking it, but by first contributing a thought. Again, touch the gray stone dust to the back of your hand when you're prepared to ask your question. But before you ask your question, with gray rock you must do this first: take these fingers, the thumb, the first finger, the second finger, and like this [he's pointing the two fingers at the rock palm down with the thumb out and the other two fingers bent down] . . . then palm up, possibly touching the back of the third finger to the rock. Touch the rock when you are prepared to give it a thought.

Only with the third finger?

No. Touch the rock like this. Touch the rock when you are prepared to give the rock a thought or even an introduction of yourself. You would introduce yourself by coming close to the rock, within an inch or two, without touching it with your fingers and thumb, and focusing on something you did that day: you got up out of bed, perhaps brushed your hair. Something simple in picture form—nothing unpleasant, just something simple you did that day. Perhaps you had breakfast or what-have-you. Or you could show a picture—meaning think of a picture—and it could be a picture of you and your spouse, or you and your parents, or you and your dog, however you want to introduce yourself. That is one way.

Because you have your hand in that direction, aimed that way toward the rock, it is an offer. It is not actually placing it in the rock, because the rock does not have to accept it. Then, if you can, have a simple uncomplicated thought—not necessarily original, but something benevolent—so the rock can understand that you are involved in engaging it in an exchange of thought. So think anything that is benevolent and pleasant, understand? Do not allow yourself to be distracted. Then touch the rock with either the picture of you and your family in your mind's eye or in your imagination. And when you have completed that, wait just a little bit, a minute, two minutes at the most. Then apply the rock dust to the back of your left hand and ask your question in the same way you did with the red rock.

4
Beige-Colored Rock and Children

Each color rock is different in terms of its properties and strengths. Now I will speak about beige-colored or tan-colored rock. When you see that rock, again follow the procedure, but you do not have to introduce yourself. That rock is enthusiastic, almost childlike. With this color rock, spontaneity is good.

I might add that beige rock celebrates children. When children are happily playing around that rock, it almost has a feeling of participation in the play. For example, when sometimes there are spirits of former residents around, still lingering for some reason, the children will almost always enter and exit your world (meaning your surface world) through that color rock because it welcomes children. It is very heart-centered and playful.

If you are to approach that rock, you can again ask your question or ask for your vision just by walking up and doing it, exactly the way a child would walk up and touch something. Do you understand? That rock is very social.

5
Remembering with Dark Brown Rock

Dark brown color always has to do with memory. You can approach dark brown rock if you have something you are trying to remember, something benevolent or anything you are attempting to remember—maybe something you saw or something you might have seen, meaning that it was a part of something else you were looking at, where you were focused in one part of your vision but there was something else happening. Sometimes it is good to try to remember things you saw out of the corner of your eye and did not think about at the time. In any event, regardless of whether the memory is pleasant or not, you can approach this rock.

Again, here you must do something besides putting the dust on the back of your left hand. I would

advise this: If you are religious, say a prayer and ask that the best come to you in the most benevolent way you can receive it. If you are spiritual or whatever your practice is, say similar words and then ask your question. Always try to ask it out loud or in some way that the physical part of your body is used, even if you have to whisper. Granted, there are some things you might not wish everyone to hear for whatever reason at any moment, so you can whisper them quietly, but there must be an audible sound. That's what I recommend.

Just to be grandfatherly for a moment, remember that it is not always good to remember everything. When you ask to remember something, make sure it's a memory from this life. And if it is something you are trying to remember from this life, be specific. If you want to remember something from a previous life, then ask that it be important to you to remember it now so you don't get bogged down in what other lives might be doing from moment to moment.

I'll tell you the hazard of that—why I'm advising you in this way. It is possible to touch in and have a vision of a previous life when that life is in the middle of doing something. Perhaps he or she is learning something or is in a drama, and the chance of you being able to touch in to find out how that drama turned out is very slight. So it might be one of those images that disturbs or distracts you or that would be hard to get out of your mind. That's why I recommend that you be very specific about what you ask for. I say again that the brown rock, the chocolate brown color, contains the memories of all it has experienced and also contains the memories of anything any other brown rock of that color has experienced anywhere on Earth, which is not always the case with other rocks. So that's another reason to be specific.

6
The Significance of Color

Are you saying that it's just the color? It has nothing to do with the chemical makeup or the name or source of the rock, just the color?

The color. I'm not saying that the consistency or the smoothness or coarseness of certain types of rocks might not be used in different ways, but I believe—and everything I have experienced supports this—that all beings choose how they look. Human beings do this, though it may not always be what services the vain or even the trends or styles of the time. It will always serve the soul's intention, however.

From what I have seen, Mother Earth is someone, and she also will choose how she looks. Rock is a portion of her body chosen to look a certain way. So in my experience, the color makes a difference. I would not rule out that if the brown rock is glassy smooth, there might be some slightly different characteristics, but it will still have to do with memory.

Wonderful! Are there any other colors here?

We've touched on the main ones in the Sedona area.

7
Soft White Rock, Strong Feelings

What about when people go home—can you expand on that? What if they go somewhere that has white rock?

We'll touch on a little bit of that. The white rock you find in some places usually has to do with feelings, strong feelings one way or another. This kind of rock is sometimes powdery—not unusual with such a rock color. It is powdery because this planet is a feeling planet, Mother Earth is a feeling being, and all who live upon her can be identified as having strong feelings. Whether humans express them or not, they have strong feelings. Even a blade of grass has strong feelings, though you may not know it. (I have checked—not with all of them, but with some—and they seem to have strong feelings.) The reason the white rock has these strong feelings is because the chances of it

becoming soft and turning to dust are strong, and in this way, it will be picked up by the wind.

Sometimes you might have wondered, reading history or science books or even storybooks, how it is possible for certain things to happen in human and animal experience all over the world at almost the same time, when people weren't communicating with one another about what they were doing—such as in the distant past when there were no telephones. How is this possible? It is possible because this powdered white rock that turns to dust easily and is picked up by the wind becomes resonant, as in a vibrating instrument, with the core of passion happening around any event, and it blows around the world.

It is surprising how quickly wind can get from one place to another carrying a particle of dust. Sometimes a few days and very often no more than a few weeks is all it takes to go around the world easily, dropping bits and pieces as the wind dies down and gusts again. So the white rock has a very important function, and that is to bring the passions of one locality to another locality—not necessarily the exact experience, not the memory of the event or whatever caused the passions or the feelings, but the feelings themselves.

That way whatever is happening on one side of the Earth can be equalized and balanced on the other side of the Earth, where it might be necessary for that place and the beings who live there to express their version of that passion. In this way, for Mother Earth—who may find it difficult herself to experience full-bodied (meaning her entire planet) passion of any one feeling, at least quickly (for Mother Earth, quickly might be a thousand years)—that passion (of an experience of humans or animals or planets or even for Mother Earth in that locality—a volcano or an earthquake, for example) needs to be on the other side of her planet quickly.

Mother Earth cannot regularly get the passion there, not in your time frame—not in a week, not in a few days—but the wind can take the powders of passion and blow them to the places where they need to be in a few days or a week. And then the beings who live there on the surface, be they plant or animal or human, will express those passions in their own way, seeding not only their own civilization with that experience, but also placing those excess passions. Passions flow out of and into other beings and other things, and humankind and animals and the plants will serve Mother Earth as they are served by her.

Whether it's chalk or marble or any white rock?

Any white rock. I will include all white rock, but the kind that is powdery to the touch is the kind most usually functioning in this way. There are other white rocks that are not so powdery, and they also might work in small grains and particles.

How does it work when the rocks get under pressure and become marble—do they still keep that quality?

You are using the science, but for me it's about color and sometimes texture. The reason I'm saying the powdery rock works best is because it is powdery. Smaller particles, actual touchable particles, can be carried by the wind in greater quantity. As a result, it is easier for the wind to take more farther, as compared to a small piece of white quartz that can go only so far.

8
The Power of White Crystals

What about white quartz? What if you are lucky enough to find a place where it's on the surface and you can talk to it?

It will have a great deal of passion. This is why some people have come to believe in the power of crystals over the years—there is, I believe, a resurgence of this belief in your time. I believe this came from other cultures that have used crystals for healing or for understanding (or what's called reading). One might hold some crystals in one's hand and move them around.

But you must remember that the white crystal is about passion and strong feelings, and if some form of healing or the stimulation of healing is involved, it is because it feels strongly. The white rock feels first,

and people who attempt to take information from white crystal will get feeling first and information second.

So understand that if you are attempting to pull information from the white crystal, there is a slight hazard. Should you have a feeling correspondent to the feeling in the white rock, its strongest feeling will come out first. It might either raise that feeling within you more, or if you have a inner feeling that can either be balanced or stimulated or even aggravated in some way by the feeling that comes out of the white rock whether you invited it or not, that will happen also. This is why in the past sometimes crystal readers have been people with strong feelings. I believe that in your time, the interest in using crystals has come from these more ancient practices, though I'm not counting clear crystal as white. White is the color white.

What about clear quartz?

I don't think of clear as a color.

9
Finding What's Lost or Hidden with Blue Stone

Since this is a book for people to take home, wherever home is, what about blue rock?

Blue? Such as? I have not seen blue rock.

I was thinking of azurite and turquoise, but there's also blue granite.

But that is not blue as we call blue. It is not the color of sky.

And azurite is actually more of a mineral than a rock.

Mineral is still a rock, yes? So azurite is a color. Where I live, there is not much blue rock, so I will look at a distance just a moment. [Pause.] The blue rock seems to have to do with the hidden, what is a secret.

I'm looking at this at a distance in the near future. I see a person walking along wearing a ring. The stone is not seated in the ring, but the ring is around the person's first finger, not the thumb. The metal around the finger is to deflect the energy of the blue stone. The blue rock is what is being used so that the person is not using his own energy from his finger. A piece of blue rock is attached to the ring, perhaps tied on with a piece of silk that conducts energy very well. This sensitive person will use the blue rock to find things that are hidden. I see this at the pyramids in twenty years or so, people using the blue rock to find things.

A dowsing instrument or something that will give you a feeling when you're close to something?

I'm not clear because I have not had personal experience. I'd say it is just that they happen to be near the pyramids. They are using it to find lost people, lost children, lost relatives—yes, I think not lost objects so much. In any event, the blue rock is about the hidden.

It's the color blue—not a particular type of rock that will help to find people, but that it's blue?

That's right. In your time, people are more attached to the type and rarity of a rock, but if you simply know the color, you can very often find a portion of a rock or a rock of that color where you live. So just remember that the blue is about the hidden, and when you are asking questions of that blue rock, you must ask very carefully so that what is revealed to you is not everything that has ever been hidden but what you wish to know for your life. Think about what to ask and what you really want to know.

Remember that you will not be presented with an answer as you often are from your computers or teachers. It will be something that you dream about or a picture that will pop into your mind, sometimes at an opportune time, other times at perhaps a more complicated time. Be alert to what you're asking for, and try to keep track of your dreams and inspirations after you ask. Remember that some rocks work more slowly than others. The brown memory rock and the blue that is the hidden work slowly, so it could come to you within three months or you might have it within a day or two.

10
A History Lesson with Black Rock

What about black rock?

Black rock has to do with history, meaning exact events as they happened everywhere. It is different than any other Earth rock. Black rock is common to many planets and even small moons. Thus, black rock can be asked about any historical event that was important to a family, a tribe, a clan, a whole nation of peoples, a whole planet of peoples or even perhaps a group of planets. You could ask the black rock in the usual way about anything that happened here or anywhere there is black rock. As far as I know, black rock is the only one, in terms of color, who can be asked about things everywhere.

11
Green Wisdom

What about green rock?

Green rock has to do with wisdom attained—not just knowledge, but wisdom—meaning a form of practice or something you do that works well for you and that you can teach others to do. Then you can ask that the rock help you, guide you, give you a vision, give you a dream, help you with your inspiration or in some way support a wisdom you wish to attain. Again, put the dust of the rock on the back of your left hand.

This information lets you have your own vision quest?

It can be helpful for people who believe in the value of individual pursuit, which in your time is perhaps a more normal experience for people than in my time. In

my time, people had to be with other people in numbers for protection because there were so many threats.

Green has to do with resonance. Resonance in this case means vibration or music. So it might be good for musicians or those involved in the music world to ask for musical inspiration. Music is universal, in my experience. No matter what the time, people have rhythmic music in some form, and on other planets, it's a very common way to communicate feelings. Sometimes people's languages are musical, even on this planet, in order to better communicate feelings. In your time, this is perhaps very important, because many people in your time are not comfortable speaking of their feelings.

12
Pink: The Color of Love Unattainable

What about if you could get close to pink rose quartz, maybe only underground, but if you could find it?

Sometimes it is found on the surface, but not often. But if you look hard, you might find it. The pink rock has to do with perception and insight, but also with something else. It has to do with love unattainable. Love unattainable means that it is not physically possible in that sense—meaning the love of God, or the love you might feel for someone in your family who has passed away and is no longer available, or a desire to have love in your life (for example, a mate not immediately attainable because you don't have him or her and you don't know where he or she is or whether

he or she is even coming into your life). So for these things, you would ask the stone in the usual way for perception or insight.

But for love unattainable, you would ask in a slightly different way. You would place your hand with your fingers opened up on your heart. Then you would put the back of your hand like that [against the rock]. Then you would ask about love unattainable, meaning that perhaps you wish to have a vision. Maybe a member of your family has died and you want to know if she is all right, if she is comfortable beyond the veil, if she is happy. That is love unattainable, because you cannot hug her anymore. Or perhaps you would like to know if you will be married someday or have a good friend, the kind of friend one loves. And so you might ask. Again, an answer is not guaranteed, but most often within three to six months at most, with love unattainable questions, something will happen. Usually—especially with someone who has passed over or died—you will get the information much quicker.

I use the word "information" because you understand it, but it is more like a vision or perhaps you will have an understanding sooner. This vision or understanding might come from the unknown or from another person. This is always the case. How many understandings and insights have you had in your life that come as a result of somebody talking with somebody else and you overheard something that was for you as well? Maybe someone is telling a story and it is about something else but it happens to touch on what you wish to know. Sometimes you won't realize you have the answer. You already know it but have almost forgotten.

13
Creator Gold

What about real gold, if you should happen to find some?

Usually, when you find a piece of real gold, it has traveled from its place of origin. So again we're talking about something that has been touched by others. If you happen to be someplace where gold is still in situ, that is exceptional. This is why there is so much gold on Earth—there really is plenty. And fortunately, there is still some left in the hills. Remember, it does not have to be a big piece, but just enough so that you can at least touch the tip of a finger to it and not be touching anything else.

Real gold stands for the vision of Creator, meaning how Creator sees you and your family or tribe, your people or nation, your planet and even your uni-

verse. Gold as it is in its natural state, in its native place, is the only color I know of that can pass this on. Now, remember, we are talking about a color, not the metal only. Sometimes you will find a gold rock that is not the mineral.

Like iron pyrite?

That's right, but it is still gold color. So you can touch that; it's the same. In this case, if it is small and you have to touch it with the small part of the back of your hand or even the back of one of your fingers of your left hand, then use the back of one of your fingertips, the fingernail. Don't use your thumb.

Do you put a little dust on it first?

If you can find it. If not, then just touch it lightly, because sometimes the dust won't be there. If you can find the dust though, the gold-colored dust, then put it on the back of your hand and touch your hand to the color. Ask, "How does Creator see me?"

It is possible in this circumstance to have a profound and mystical experience. You might in that moment see many faces of yourself in different lives, or you might get a picture or a symbol that comes strongly to you or be overwhelmed by a feeling. It would be a good feeling. You might have an experience that you would only later realize is the vision, the picture of how Creator sees you. Just know that this is profound. Creator will never give you an ugly vision of how It sees you. What I mean by ugly is not appearance, but rather something that is unpleasant or violent—it will not be that.

14
Dreaming in Purple

What about amethyst, if you could get close to a lavender or purple rock?

Purple has to do with dreams. Dreams in my time meant dreams at night during sleep. But dreams in your time also mean hopes, what you might wish for or hope for. I'm using hope to make it more clear, not necessarily to be more defined. But it also has to do with what you might dream about.

Again, say you have lost someone you love for whatever reason; you might be able to follow the usual procedure with the purple. Ask to have a pleasant dream about this lost love, in which case you might have the dream. Ask also to remember the parts of the dream that will help you to feel better about this.

Will this also work for lighter colors?

It works for dark and medium purple, but not light purple so much.

15
All the Colors of the World

So those are the colors. If someone comes to Sedona and asks to be shown a place or tries to find a place where his heart feels good—is there anything else that person can do in Sedona that will help him on the spiritual path?

Remember, stone is not the only source of color. Wherever you are, there is the color of the sky. Sometimes it is white, sometimes blue, sometimes darker shades. If you live someplace where stone is not available—such as in a big city—use the sky. Use the white light from the stars at night or from the Moon. Reach toward it with the back of your hand. Even though you cannot put starlight on the back of your hand, you can pretend. Reach up with your other hand and gather starlight. Rub it on the back of your hand and act as if it were the stone, for the star is something that may be partly stone, wherever it is.

So if you are in a city or someplace where you can't go to the rock, utilize the natural color of something else. Clouds in the sky are white also, or use the color of blue sky. Even if you can't touch it, reach for it as if you could. When you reach for it as if you could touch it, even without knowing what you are doing, you will use the long reach, the long touch that is a mystical technique. You must reach for the sky, though, from good heart, meaning something you want or need to know for yourself or others that will benefit you or others—that is good heart.

16
Water's Feminine Reflection

You can also do this with water. Water always shows others more about themselves; that is why water reflects. And remember, water represents feminine energy on Earth. This tells you something about women. Women and the feminine energy always show others hints about themselves. In my time, a tribe that lacks or has lost its mystical people will always choose a woman first to perform mystical work. If they know the woman isn't available or it seems like she can't do mystical work, then the second choice is the man. But always with the mystical work, the first choice is the woman because she reflects something that will tell others about themselves. That is at the core of the feminine energy and is represented here with water.

If you are on a ship at sea and there are no rocks around, look over the edge of the ship at the water. Maybe you won't see yourself, but you can reach for the water just like you reached for the sky. Day or night, you can reach and ask the water in its infinite colors of reflection. With the back of your left hand, ask it to show you something good about yourself: "Show me something good about myself please, if you would, woman of water."

Then, you see, you are specific—"something good." Maybe you have a problem that needs to be resolved; maybe you have talents you don't know are talents; maybe there is something good about you that you have forgotten and others know about. Perhaps you will be reminded so you feel better about yourself. You don't have to ask anyone to show you things about yourself that are not so good, because life has a way of doing that to you and you don't need help.

I can see a picture of zillions of people who live on the coasts of countries in high apartment buildings . . .

That's right.

17
Rocks by the Sea and Inner Insight

You started to talk about how different it was to touch a rock that ocean waves had touched.

Say there is a rock outcropping near the sea. If the sea touches it, then the rock's color abilities will be heightened. Remember, you are human beings, and ultimately any question you ask will have to do with who you are or what you do, mostly about yourself, even if it is about your people, the group you are part of. The water touching the rock, even though it seems to change the color momentarily, will make that color of rock better for that instant. So if you want to go to rocks by the sea, they will often work better for insights associated with yourself.

18
Touching Sedona

When you are planning a trip to Sedona, find things to do for everyone in the family, but you yourself are maybe going to have a day when you can do these spiritual things for yourself. Go around touching the colors of the stones and things that appeal to you spiritually, and think about what questions you will ask. Maybe you could write things down, but you will have to make the time so that when you come, you will know what to ask, even if it takes awhile to find out where to go. You might not be able to remember all the colors and what they mean, but because this book is small and portable, you can put it in your pocket or your purse and carry it with you.

When you go to the creek with the children and they are playing in the water, sit by the shore. If you see some rock, touch it and ask your question. Follow the procedure and ask the question. Then give yourself a moment afterward to rest. If you don't have a moment to rest, then repeat the procedure. The moment to rest or relax afterward—anything from a minute to three minutes or more—is very important. This is not a time to dwell on other thoughts but to let the question go.

The way to let your question go is to look at other things. You can watch your children in the water, but don't worry about them; you don't want to get into feelings of worry. You just want to experience beauty for the minute or three minutes or more after you have asked your question. And the easiest way to do that in Sedona or other places of beauty is to look around you. Look at the mountains, look at the sky over the mountains, at the red rock, the water—look at whatever is beautiful. If your children are beautiful and you don't worry when you look at them, look at them.

The main thing you want to feel for these first minutes is beauty; this will help you to let go of what you have asked for. Because if you hold on to it and think about it and worry about it, the color of the stone will not be able to help you because you haven't given the question to the stone. If you're going to give it to the stone, you must actually give it and then let it go. You can't hang on after you have given it. And then you will be done. Go on with your life. Go have a good time, play and don't think about it. It will come to you when it is the right time.

19
A Benevolent Offering

What about the issue of offering something? A visitor to Sedona probably won't have something alive with them, but what about making an offering of corn or something?

Well, the question is the offering. Asking for something means you have faith. You ask the stone. You say, "I trust you have something to give me, and here is what I'm giving you: respect, honor and appreciation for your beauty. And I ask, if it's easy for you"—don't say that, but it's implied—"if it is easy for you, then perhaps you can give me some beauty from what I asked."

If people are mystical or spiritual and they wish to make an offering, then the offering must be benevolent—meaning if it is cornmeal, it must be corn you have raised. It can't just be cornmeal you buy at the store. It has to be something personal to you, that you have sung to. Or it could be other material that you use to make food. But the reason cornmeal is traditionally used is that it is a personal sacrifice. In your time, of course, that would not be so easy to do. So I'd say that if people are of traditional spiritual nature, they will know what to offer—spiritual meaning in the sense that they will know what to offer.

Appendix A
Sedona Rock Beings

Another fascinating thing to do in Sedona is to find the images in the rocks. Here are some examples of photos taken by the photographer Mirtala of some of Sedona's rock beings.

Profiles

Sarawati

Two Figures

Lion's Head

Queen

Dragon

Sphinx

Dancing Figures

Sedona Vortex Guide Book

Various Authors

A unique and in-depth examination of some of the reasons that draw four million people to Sedona every year.

$14.95 SOFTCOVER 236 P.

ISBN 0-929385-25-X

Feeling Sedona's ET Energies

Zoosh though Robert Shapiro

- Boynton Canyon
- Schnebly Hill
- Cathedral Rock
- Long Canyon
- Airport Vortex
- West Fork
- Bell Rock
- Feel the Energies

$9.95 SOFTCOVER 68 P.

ISBN 1-891824-46-5

LIGHT Technology PUBLISHING

1-800-450-0985 • www.lighttechnology.com

Book 1

Benevolent Magic & Living Prayer

Channeled through Robert Shapiro

An introduction to the feminine science of benevolent magic and living prayer and what they can do for you. A chapter on how the processes work and many examples of specific words to say that will enable you to create a benevolent life for yourself and others—here and now.

$9.95 SOFTCOVER
ISBN 1-891824-49-X

LIGHT Technology PUBLISHING

1-800-450-0985 • www.lighttechnology.com

Book 2

Disentanglement & Deep Disentanglement

Channeled through Robert Shapiro

$9.95 SOFTCOVER

ISBN 1-891824-48-1

Book 3

Disengagement, Engagement & Connections

Channeled through Robert Shapiro

$9.95 SOFTCOVER

ISBN 1-891824-49-X

LIGHT Technology PUBLISHING

1-800-450-0985 • www.lighttechnology.com

Living in the Heart

CD WITH HEART MEDITATION INCLUDED!

Drunvalo Melchizedek

"Long ago we humans used a form of communication and sensing that did not involve the brain in any way; rather, it came from a sacred place within our heart. What good would it do to find this place again in a world where the greatest religion is science and the logic of the mind? Don't I know this world where emotions and feelings are second-class citizens? Yes, I do. But my teachers have asked me to remind you who you really are. You are more than a human being, much more. For within your heart is a place, a sacred place where the world can literally be remade through conscious cocreation. If you give me permission, I will show you what has been shown to me."

$25.00 SOFTCOVER 120 P.

ISBN 1-891824-43-0

LIGHT Technology PUBLISHING

1-800-450-0985 • www.lighttechnology.com

Dimensional Journey
Encounters and Teachings

Linda Ball

Linda openly talks about her experiences on Bradshaw Ranch.

$19[95] SOFTCOVER 143 P.
ISBN 1-891824-34-1

Ultimate UFO Series:
Andromeda

The Andromedans and Zoosh through Robert Shapiro

Including the complete, orignal text of the Wendelle Stevens book, *UFO Contact from Andromeda: Extraterrestrial Prophecy*

The Andromedans who contacted the Professor speak through Robert Shapiro.

$16[95] SOFTCOVER 459 P.
ISBN 1-891824-35-X

LIGHT Technology PUBLISHING

1-800-450-0985 • www.lighttechnology.com

SEDONA

Journal of EMERGENCE!

Rated Number One!

We Offer Answers to Satisfy the Heart and to Inspire Lives!

The *Sedona Journal of Emergence!* is the one monthly magazine readers never throw away. It features predictions that discuss what's happening right now, this day, this month, and how you can make the most of the potentials created by the acceleration of frequency in your life on every level—physical, mental, emotional, spiritual—and on the integrated levels of wholeness that are becoming possibilities now. It even offers your very own personal horoscope for each week of the month.

The *Sedona Journal* also contains the latest channeled information on what to do as humans and the Earth move from the third to the fourth dimension and reveals how these energies affect you and the Earth. No other monthly magazine offers the quantity and quality of guidance by other-dimensional beings, not only to help you through these unprecedented times, but to help you make sense of and understand what all of this opening and expansion means to you!

The *Sedona Journal* is filled with practical articles, and features on ETs, UFOs, herbs, minerals, dreams, the tarot, healing, numerology, reincarnation and more!

ELECTRONIC SUBSCRIPTIONS available for SJE!

$43/YEAR for 12 issues

$77/2 YEARS for 24 issues!

Must be puchased online at: www.sedonajournal.com for you to obtain a user name and password.

Get the latest channeling and astrology two weeks before it is available on the newsstand.

1-800-450-0985 • WWW.LIGHTTECHNOLOGY.COM